Anežka Česká

Agnes of Bohemia

by

JAROMÍR HOŘEC

Translated into the English by Jana Morávková Kiely

Červená Barva Press
Somerville, Massachussets

Červená Barva Press
P.O. Box 440357
W. Somerville, MA 02144-3222

www.cervenabarvapress.com

Bookstore: www.thelostbookshelf.com

Cover Art and Book Illustrations: Lumír Šindelář

Cover photo: Prague Castle and part of Charles bridge by night in Prague, Czech Republic by Karel Jakubec

Cover Design: William J. Kelle

ISBN: 978-0-578-02262-8

For my Mother

Table of Contents

Introduction: A long awaited miracle

In September 2000, I found a copy of *Anežka Česká*, a collection of poems by Jaromír Hořec, in my mother's house in France. My mother had just died at the age of 92. I was touched by Lumír Šindelář's illustrations and took the book home with me to Cambridge, Massachusetts. A year or so later, missing my frequent phone calls and my visits to my mother, I was perusing my bookshelf and came upon *Anežka Česká* again. As I began to read, the sound of rich, beautiful Czech surrounded me, as if my mother was holding me in her arms. I went to sleep that night filled to the brim with the music of the poetry. Smetana's, *Má Vlast* and Dvořák's *New World Symphony* seemed to be humming, together with verses from the poems, in my dreams. In the morning, I realized the poetry was still with me, but this time, I was hearing it in English. I decided to put down what I heard and that's how I began to translate *Anežka Česká* into *Agnes of Bohemia*.

My mother had bought the book in Rome in November 1989 where she had gone with my sister for the canonization of Anežka Česká, Agnes of Bohemia, sometimes also called Agnes of Prague. From all over the world, men and women with Czech and Slovak roots, gathered in Rome to celebrate an event that had been part of their country's history and legends for seven hundred years.

Anežka was a Czech princess born in Prague, to King Přemysl Otakar I. and Queen Konstancie, on January 20th 1208. Her father, as a true Přemyslid, was a strong, ambitious man. Her mother, a relative of St. Elisabeth of Hungary, was known for her gentleness and deep piety.

Historical as well as literary sources show Anežka as a beautiful young woman, with her father's strength and her mother's gentleness and sensitivity to others. A highly educated woman, she spoke Czech, German and Latin, writing letters and listening to troubadours' songs in these languages.

As a child, Anežka and her sister Anna were sent to live for three years with their Aunt Hedwig in the Cistercian monastery of Třebonice. Later she spent a year in a Premonstratian monastery near Prague and five years in Vienna. Monasteries were the centers of learning and cradles of Western civilization. Through the monastic liturgy, and the Bible, particularly the ancient poetry of the Book of Psalms, the Psalter was the daily food of her mind and heart.

Anežka was highly influenced by two of her contemporaries, Saints Francis and Claire of Assisi, who though from wealthy families gave up their possessions to go and serve the poorest of the poor. Thousands of young people in Italy and throughout Europe followed them. Anežka deeply admired and made her own the Franciscan ideals of love, joy, peace, meekness and gentleness; joyful thanksgiving for creation and acceptance of personal suffering; active, loving care of the needy and respect for every creature. The first Franciscan friars had appeared in Prague around the time of her birth. By the time she was ten years old, the fame of Francis and Claire had spread throughout Europe.

As was the custom, Princess Anežka was used by her father as a pawn in the game of political alliances and from the age of nine, betrothed, several times, first to a German prince, then to the son of the Emperor, and finally to the King of England. For reasons, that included the untimely death of her fiancé, as well as complicated, political machinations, the first three betrothals came to naught. Through her great inner strength, her faith and her independence of spirit, she was not broken by what proved to be bitter experiences of exile and humiliation.

Eventually the Holy Roman Emperor, Frederic II, himself asked for her hand. By then, Anežka's father had died and her brother Václav, who loved her very much, was king. She was not bound by filial obedience to him.

Resolved to help her peace loving homeland, impoverished by wars and the profligacy of its rulers, she became more and more certain of her vocation to follow the example of Francis and Claire. She kept a correspondence with Claire, as well as Pope Gregory IX, a friend of Francis, regarding her plans to reject the marriage offer from the Emperor, and join the Order of the Poor Clares in Prague. With the Pope's support, she succeeded. Seven noble

Czech young women followed her into the poverty of the Franciscan life. They joined five sisters who had been sent by Claire from Assisi.

Anežka persuaded her brother King Václav I, to build a monastery where she was made abbess. She built a hospital for the poor in Prague, on the shores of the river Vltava, which remained in operation until 1945. She worked there herself, washing, cleaning, cooking, and caring for the sick. Later, she founded the Order of the Crusaders of the Red Star, the only religious order of Czech origin, dedicated to helping victims of the plague. (All of her buildings, though altered along the centuries, can still be seen in the vicinity of the Charles Bridge and the new Four Seasons Hotel.)

At the height of a particularly difficult crisis which had split the land in two, with civil war looming between two factions, one led by her brother, King Vaclav, and by his son Přemysl Otakar, Anežka succeeded in bringing the feuding parties together in her monastery and brokering peace between them. She died on March 2, 1287, at the age of 74, having already become a legend, a lasting symbol of peace and reconciliation.

Her cause of canonization (i.e. the process of being proclaimed a saint of the universal Church in Rome) was initiated by popular demand in 1328. But it took more than seven hundred years and a Slavic pope, John Paul II, for Anežka to be finally canonized. The official reason for the delay was that her body could not be found. But other more likely obstacles to the process had developed along the way: The burning in 1415, at the Council of Constance of hero, scholar, and reformer Jan Hus, fused Czech patriotism with the Hussite cause provoking two hundred years of Hussite wars against Rome and its allies. This was followed by the collaboration of the Czech Catholic Church of the Counter-Reformation with Germanizing elements during the time of annexation of Czech Lands to the Austro-Hungarian Empire. The tensions created would not be resolved until the twentieth century.

Another, earlier reason might also have been the tragic and politically awkward story of Anežka's sister Vilemína, who had the courage to demand the equality of women with men in theCatholic

Church. She had moved to Rome and founded a community working towards that end. Completely ignored during her lifetime, after her death, her body and all her writings were burnt and her ashes scattered by order of Church authorities. (see Hořec's poem, *Whenever Fire*)

The beatification, the first official step towards the canonization of Anežka, took place in 1881, her cult having grown together with the national and cultural nineteenth century Czech revival. The delay in her canonization lead to the legendary prophecy: "When Anežka is at last canonized a great blessing will come upon her land." And so it happened. She was canonized on November 12, 1989, one week before the Velvet Revolution, which brought a peaceful end to sixty years of repression under Nazi, then Soviet, totalitarian regimes.

As president Václav Havel put it the following year, in his now famous speech welcoming John Paul II to Prague:

"I don't know if I know what is a miracle. Yet, I dare say, that at this moment I am a participant in a miracle: To a land devastated by the ideology of hate, comes the herald of love, to a land devastated by the rule of illiterate philistines, comes the living symbol of culture, to a land until recently wrecked by ideas of world confrontation and division, comes the herald of peace, dialogue, mutual tolerance, respect and understanding, bearing tidings of fraternal unity within diversity."

For me, this miracle marked the first time I could return home to Bohemia (Čechy) since 1948, when I had to leave it suddenly at the age of ten, and go into exile with my family. We lived in France, Morocco, Germany, Switzerland. Eventually, I came to Harvard University as a graduate student. It is then that I met my husband, soon to become a professor of English literature there. On one of our first dates, on the "singing beach" in Manchester by the sea, he read to me in Italian from a book very close to his heart, *The Little Flowers of St Francis*. A year later, we went to Assisi on our honeymoon. Our love affair with Francis and Claire had started together with our own and has continued throughout our lives. "What is this about your family and St. Francis?" One of our children's friends remarked when visiting our house in New Hampshire. "He is in every room." "And that's not all!" our youngest daughter chimed in. "Each one of us has either Francis or Claire in his or her name."

By the time I discovered Jaromír Hořec's *Anežka Česká*, my husband and I had been back to Assisi and the many Franciscan places throughout Italy countless times. Each time we would discover some new and delightful detail about Francis, Claire or one of their companions. Slowly, through many adventures and a great deal of reading, we began to get glimpses of the extraordinary power for good of the Franciscan spirit around the world.

And Hořec's beautiful poetry brought everything I loved together: a Bohemian princess from my childhood home of Prague, who kept a correspondence with St. Claire of Assisi regarding her own vocation to join the Franciscan movement; a princess so impressed by the life of the *poverello* that she was willing to set aside both her own crown and the one offered to her by the Holy Roman Emperor in order to become a servant of the poor.

I translated Hořec's first two poems, *Gentleness nestled in her* and *So patiently did she address the flowers of the fields*, with joyful ease. They are a lovely introduction of Anežka as a person, as well as an elegant rendition of the Franciscan ideal.

The tone of the third poem, *O Mother Tongue*, surprised me at first. Was Hořec returning to the nineteenth century struggle for the survival of Czech language, and if so, why? The theme resurfaced in a later poem, *Mother of Seven Sorrows*, and I understood then the contemporary struggle Hořec was alluding to. I knew from personal experience how easy it would be to lose a language and how much would be lost with it. After I finished high school in Casablanca and went to Paris to study at the Sorbonne, it would have been so much easier to write to my parents, who were still in Morocco, in French. Yet I felt that writing in anything else but Czech would have shaken our relationship out of the realm of primal affection and deepest truth. As it was, I often mixed in my letters Czech and French. My mother corrected these, sending them back with grammatical explanations attached. I knew from my parents how important it had been for us as a people to keep up our native tongue. Preserving the language, in spite of endless attacks on it, was above all what made Czechs and Slovaks able in 1918 to regain their independence after three hundred years of subservience in the Austro-Hungarian Empire! Translating *Anežka* made me understand at last what great gift my parents had given me. I could see the extraordinary treasure that lies in a language. Being able to play with several languages at the same time, I felt I could reach that mysterious connection between words and movements of the soul, the soul of my people. I was deeply grateful.

In the next poem, (*In her heart anguished darkness*) the theme of darkness appeared for the first time. It was a darkness I could understand. Like Anežka, I had to go into exile and leave behind people I loved. Like her, I was taken to foreign lands, where people spoke languages I did not understand and ate food I was not used to eating. Like her, I felt terribly homesick. I imagined her looking up with awe at the magnificent primeval border forests, a national treasure, legendary in her time and still standing in 1948 when I, in turn, passed through them. Soon after, they were heavily damaged especially after the Soviet invasion of 1968.

For the first half of the book, it was easy to feel the substance of the poems in a very personal way: the painful encounter of a young, highly educated, idealistic girl with the corruption of those who held power (*Is this the bright light of betrothal*), the absolute determination not to become one of them (*Even If*), the hope that in the midst of it all true love may be hiding *(Milostna)*, the turning to God for help in prayer *(Bless by your light and The very stones joined their hands in prayer)*, and finally, the giving of one's whole life over to God (*The Consecration*) in order to become a light for others (*A lamp of hope*) and an instrument of peace and reconciliation for her people (*Reconciliation*).

The theme of darkness returned and predominated throughout the poems in the second half of the book, (*The Exiles, Children of death*) and culminated in *Mother of Seven Sorrows* and *A Hundred Hearts began to beat.* Here was a primary example of dissident literature. The poems ostensibly described the pitiful state of the Czech Lands after what is known as one of the greatest tragedies of Czech history, the defeat and death of the young King Přemysl Otakar II at the Moravian Field in 1278. But they are, above all, a description of the ecological disaster and economic and moral collapse during the "normalization" which followed the Soviet occupation in 1968. The poet's empassioned lines about the Mother tongue in *Mother of Seven Sorrows*, describes how, in order to prove the working class origins which alone would assure them jobs and freedom from persecussion, people had to use a rough, unimaginative, uneducated language, which for that time became standard Czech. One of the attractions of poets like Hořec, as well as the leadership power of the playwright Václav Havel, came from their willful use, their resurrection, so to speak, of the poetic Czech language once again. It seemed like an unexpected 20th century revival of the long nineteenth century struggle for the preservation of the language.

I found the darkest poems of *Anežka Česká* very hard to translate and turned, for a time, to the letters of St. Claire to Anežka. Anežka's letters to Claire have not been kept, but four of Claire's letters to Anežka, on the other hand, have been preserved and are among the only six known documents written by Claire to have survived to this day. Precious texts of great beauty, they reveal Claire's poetic soul, a true sister soul to that of Francis, full of radiant joy and peace. They also reveal her great admiration and love for Anežka. In Claire's first letter to Anežka, Agnes of Bohemia, she writes:

"As I hear of the fame of your holy conduct and irreproachable life, which is known not only to me but to the entire world as well, I greatly rejoice and exult in the Lord...For though you, more than others, could have enjoyed the magnificence and honor and dignity of the world, and could have been married to the illustrious Caesar with splendor befitting You and His Excellency. You have rejected all these things and have chosen with your whole heart and soul a life of holy poverty...Thus you took a spouse of a more noble lineage."

And in the second letter:

"Place your mind before the mirror of eternity!
Place your soul in the brilliance of glory!
Place your mind in the figure of the divine substance!
And transform your whole being into the image of
The Godhead itself
Through contemplation!
So that you may feel what His friends feel
As they taste the hidden sweetness
Which God himself has reserved
From the beginning
For those who love Him!"

For the poet Pope John Paul II, Claire's letters became a fitting substitute for Anežka's missing body.

Hořec's poetic versions of the letters (*First Letter of Claire on Poverty, Second Letter about Christ, Third Letter about Pride of the Powerful, Fourth Letter about the Defiant Birch Tree,*) are very much in Claire's spirit, yet quite different. The last may be the loveliest of all the poems.

Finding it hard to return to the theme of darkness, I might have given up the translation altogether had it not been for the encouragement of my friend Daria Donnelly, Associate Editor of *Commonweal.* She was going through painful treatments for terminal cancer. Yet her spirit seemed to triumph over it, like that of Anežka triumphing over the darkness in her land. She suggested I contact Jaromír Hořec to ask for permission to translate the book.

By then it was 2004. I called Jaromír Hořec in Prague, explaining I would like to meet him and get his official blessing for the translation of *Anežka Česká.* He was elated. The story had long been put aside in the Czech Republic, but now some lady from America suddenly remembered and was trying to bring it back to life again. It seemed like another miracle.

I met him in Prague outside of Café Slavia by the Vltava River. I found a white haired, not very tall, pleasant looking man with burning eyes, dressed in a dark overcoat, clutching a thin, black briefcase. I followed him as he walked with his back very straight inside the café and lead me through the maze of tables until he found a place for us. "There," he said, showing the table across from us, where a couple, clearly very much in love and with not a care in the world, seemed to be enjoying each other's company. "That's where we used to sit. The "dissidents" you know. We knew the table was bugged. We played word games to distract the weasels." The humor in his tone was typically Czech. I knew this is how they survived. The awful situation was bearable only with the help of thousands of political jokes, jumping like little sparks from person to person. Even these could bring you a lot of trouble if overheard by an informer. Slowly the humor became darker and darker. But even humor was not enough to bear the darkness of "normalization."

I wanted the poet to tell me what prompted him to compose *Anežka*. His face changed. He looked straight at me. "I wrote *Anežka* in a period of utter darkness in our lives," he said earnestly, then stopped, looking at me with questioning eyes. He wondered whether I could ever understand what he meant, whether I, a woman from America sitting across from him, who had suddenly appeared amidst the brightness of newly restored Prague, could ever fathom what they all had gone through.

No/ Cries every vein/ recoiling in disgust/ ...   Perjurers claim fidelity/ ... Judges mock justice/ ...Embezzlers are raised/ to ill famed honors...(Even If)

A uncompromising *no* was what it took to sign Charter 77, a document drawn up by Czechoslovak dissidents demanding that the government of the Czechoslovak Socialist Republic actually observe the 1975 Helsinki Accords on human rights, which it had ratified. Most people were dissidents in their minds, but very few had the courage to sign the document. Jaromír Hořec was one of those who did sign at a time when signing meant loss of job, starvation for you and your family (if not for the help of friends,) inability for your children to continue their education, prison.

Even if...complete darkness surrounded me/ nothing would turn away my steps/ nothing in this world, the poet cried through Anežka as he, like her turned away from *this world which worships itself* and decided to follow *the faithful/ barefoot and poor/ living on spring water and forest fruit (Even If)*.

"Writing *Anežka* was for me light in the darkness," the poet continued, his face brightening as if remembering his hymn to Anežka in *Slender Flame*:

Slender Flame…With your rays you tame darkness/ Persistent as Marah's bitter waters/ …
Taking under your wings all God's creatures/ …Woman/ abounding in purity/ daybreak/ Gentle mother/ compassionate/ Slender Flame.

But Hořec did not want to talk about his time in prison, except to admit that it was there that *Anežka* was conceived. He did wish to talk about his experience during the Velvet Revolution:

"I could not participate in the demonstrations. (He had come out of prison with broken health.) On November 27th 1989, I was sick in bed. The government had forbidden all coverage of the demonstrations. I turned on my television by chance. Suddenly, on the screen, I saw it all happening, an enormous crowd. I heard verses read! It was my poetry and people were going wild."

Už aby byli pryč
Už aby svědomí nehladovělo v celách
Už aby Anežka Česká požehnala své zemi
Už abychom se mohli podívat Bohu do očí
že jsme se nezpronevěřili.

Let them be gone..
Let conscience starve in prison cells no more
May Anežka Česká at last bless her land
That we may look God straight in the eye
And see that we had not betrayed him

I was deeply moved. It was clear as I looked into the poet's eyes this had been a moment worth waiting and suffering for.

I heard accounts of the Velvet Revolution not only from Hořec, but from many friends and relatives who had been there throughout.

In January 1989, demonstrations took place at the spot of the self-immolation of Jan Palach, a student who burned himself to death in 1969 in protest against the Soviet invasion. These demonstrations were immediately and harshly put down. Fear tightened its grip over the land. While Solidarnost was growing, Tianmen Square unfolding, the Berlin Wall crumbling, nothing seemed to be happening in Czechoslovakia.

Finally in November came the canonization. Thousands of Czechs and Slovaks traveled to Rome in spite of endless difficulties put up by the government. There they met many of those who had been in exile and had come there from the four corners of the world. All of Rome seemed to be speaking Czech. "It suddenly seemed possible," my mother and sister told me, "that Czechoslovaks could again come together in peace and freedom."

In Prague, many of those who could not make it to Rome attended mass at the cathedral, in honor of Anežka's canonization. As the crowds poured out from the cathedral, the archbishop of Prague, Cardinal František Tomášek, supported by John Paul II himself, stepped outside and called out: "I am with you." There was a hugely enthusiastic response and the crowds marched down from the castle singing.

Soon after, a demonstration allowed by the government, commemorating the death of Jan Opletal, killed by the Nazis during the German occupation, turned into a peaceful but forceful demand for freedom and justice. Police were called to stop it. They cornered the student procession on Národní Třída and began to wield their sticks. Many students were severely beaten. Young people ran down towards the theaters. Plays were interrupted and turned into impassioned speeches for freedom, solidarity and human rights.

From then on demonstrations took place every day. "We would go to work," a doctor friend of mine told me. "After work we would join the crowds on St. Václav Square and start shaking our keys, ringing out the end of the Communist regime. It began near the statue of St. Václav, by the sacred place where Jan Palach had burnt himself. Every day crowds got larger. We would eventually meet our whole family there and all our neighbors too."

The crowds on St. Václav's square got not only larger, but more and more varied. Musicians like Marta Kubišová, Michal Kocáb, Vladimir Merta, and hundreds of others who had been silenced since 1969, or like Karel Kryl, who had been exiled, reappeared and were welcomed as heroes. Others, like the singer Dagmar Andrtová, forced by the government to become a street cleaner during "normalization," went on the road throughout the countryside to ask people, uninformed because of media black out, to join the revolution in Prague. Poets whose work had been banned read their poetry aloud from balconies. Speeches by Dubček and other leaders of the Prague Spring, as well as Havel and other Charter 77 signers followed one another, everyone at last able to speak the truth openly.

The crowds got so numerous that the demonstrations had to be moved to the larger space above the castle called Letná. It was then that the young dissident priest, Václav Malý, read Hořec's verses as a wish of the people. And as the media black out was suddenly overcome the whole nation could hear the words:

"Let conscience starve in prison cells no more
May Anežka Česká at last bless her land."

After that, the chief of the police group who had beaten the students stood up to publicly apologize. Could the apology of a policeman, even a police chief, make up for the crimes of forty-one years of a police state? A jumble of dissonant murmurs was heard from the crowd. Then, Fr. Václav Malý took the microphone again and asked: "Will you accept his apology?" An extraordinary silence spread over Letná and lasted what seemed liked an eternity. Finally, slowly, slowly, a new murmur, rhythmical, like a wave, grew stronger and stronger: *"Od..pou..štíme…od..pou..štíme…"* *"We for-give-you, We for-give- you…"* "No other moment in my life has ever equaled this one," many of those who were there, told me.

When the wave died down, Fr. Malý asked the crowd to recite the *Our Father* together. Everyone knew the miracle had happened. Anežka had blessed her land and once again brought about a peaceful reconciliation. The Communist government resigned. On December 10th, a new government was sworn in and Václav Havel was elected president.

—Jana Morávková Kiely

Anežka Česká

Agnes of Bohemia

Gentleness Nestled in Her

Gentleness nestled in her
it came to her
at dawn
in silence
over dew

- Listen to the night rain with your whole heart
while paging through the Psalter
Let every little stone
be your brother
Bend down to the poor daisies
and with every little spark
above every soil
drink the singing air

-Humbly accept pain
walk towards it barefoot through thorns
You will be radiant
as you lay on the wounds of others
your own suffering
raise up the stumbling and the wretched
pardon prisoners
and build a refuge from the darkness of plague
on the shores of the royal river
that God unfurled at the feet of Prague.

-Never tie yourself to slavery of spirit
or sacrifice to power
or give in to worldly glory
that blinds those who do see

She spoke so patiently to the flowers of the fields

She spoke so patiently to the flowers of the fields
so ardently
at last she coaxed them into speech

In muddy dumps
where entrance is forbidden
a blue light spreads
as if the sky had walked there at dawn

-From wanderers she hears:
Allow apple skins to ripen
Give weather time to clear

Verbasca blaze like
royal torches
kindled by the sun
On the steep slopes of their sovereignties

-As for you be mindful of yourself
avoid the scepters of homage
The true lampstand alone
lift up
the light of truth

From Konstancie' s hands
Accepting the word:
      -Be like a gentle mist to misery
      sicknesses and blind souls
      Soften their darkness
      And your crippled native land
      clasp tightly to your heart

That is your destiny

O Mother Tongue

Words of a soft rose
wafted about her
she wished to touch that unreal complexion
and keep near her lips its freshness
its firmament of comely light

Resting at first in darkness
the seed of mother tongue
bathed in sun rays and rain
sprouted at last into the greenery
of the earth at daybreak

O mother tongue
most delectable tonic
of the air we breathe
pulsing with blood
the moon lights your jeweled vault by night
and showers gifts on your faithful ones

Within cloister walls
in the glow of her silence
the Scriptures opened
in which God opposes evil
and calls the lowliest to himself

From illuminations
heavenly azure descends towards her
and the song of letters
lifts the wings of solitude

In the midst of bird songs she read
the first Czech word-
Milost- (Grace, Loveliness, Compassion)

In her heart anguished darkness

By night burning knives
border the road
immersed to the hilt in the blood of lambs
Wolves on every side

Still the Vltava
washes dust from her feet
in the shades of ferns
Border forests still
whisper in her dreams
She still hears matins in Czech
but already out of the mists over the rye
sacrificial stones have arisen
where they mixed
human blood with that of beasts

They are taking her to pagan hearths
where idols beat their breasts
and for their gratification
drink bottoms up tubs of tears
She is riding bound to the slaughter
her mouth not to belong to her
they sold her
seeing is forbidden
the clarity of words is silenced
in her heart anguished darkness

And her own prayers?
Hushed as if by sickness from an evil eye

Or else

Or else
as was allotted to Isaac?
On the mountain in the land of Moriah
to blaze up in sacrifice
in obedience to God

But what sense is there in my destruction
what purpose can it serve
as fire and sword are raised
by strayed armed altar men?

Has even the angel of the Lord
been struck dumb?
Will he appear at the last moment?
Will he hold back the sacrificial knife
and cry:
Do not raise your hand against the child
do not harm her?

Is it your justice
God
I do not understand?
Your anger against me
Did you let me be bound hand and foot?

Have mercy
Bless father
That he may clasp me to himself again
And bring me back to the silence of the brightest of days
where mother
and my singing sisters
already await me.

Is this the bright light of betrothal?

Is this the bright light of betrothal
this unsanctified mire?

The deference of pipers sounds
at the very bottom of drunken waters
-Over here a hindquarter of lechery!
Yells through the shutters the gluttonous court
- A pitcher of rage
- A platter full of cruelty
Leopold Babenberg is ready to traffic in the temple
- Fill up with treason
- This hatred is not cooked enough
- Spread those thighs!
From German throats
whores hung with brocades and plundered jewels
a draught of horse stable

Debauched prelates bestow their blessings
stuffing themselves on fast days
lies reeking from their throats
Your real name Vindobona
be Sodoma

Heaven's wrath will scorch these sins
and the lustful shrieks of the powerful
Not a single righteous
can be found in this wasteland
where only pillars of salt will smolder in the darkness

And Henry VII ?
The serene king of Sicily
Roman ruler
rather Satan's emperor
pledged in blood to mire and drunkenness

What do they want to add to my chains?
What did they agree on?

Thirty thousand marks of silver
from father
and fifteen more promised by
uncle Ludwig of Bavaria

I am only to be thrown into the bargain with the dowry
The dealers drink
through burning nights
to my end

    -Margaret worm yourself among them
     You belong together
     I shall open the door
     To your insatiable fornication

Follow the will
of these forsworn evildoers
croaking in the swamps?
Wander along erratic boulders
towards the voluptuousness of a sovereign
among foreigners
Who don't understand the Word?
My lot:
The Czech Lands

Exult until you choke all Henry's company
and wail in your pleasures
I'd rather heal the lowly
than blindly gratify godlessness
I am not one of you
To minions of baseness
a Přemyslovna
will not be a maid

Your name Konstancie

Your name does not fade
not even within foreign walls
in the midst of one's own miseries
where vanity forlorn
pounds the stones

Your name mother
drowns the fluttering banners
It is more powerful than bloody baldachins
than dazzling jewels
on provocative necks
Fiefdoms of worldly rulers
next to it
are but a handful of ashes

The glow of piety wells up from its music
and persists on the vault of heaven gripped by darkness
forcing loneliness to its knees

A healing philter
to anguish
Graciously breezy
in Hungarian
Charming in enchanting Polish
royal
when pronounced by the Lady of Germania
But loveliest of all
in the chimes of Czech

An illuminating spray
mother
your name Konstancie

Whenever fire

Whenever fire bursts out of the ground
she reaches for it
let pain burn her

In her prayers
she blasphemes her own gentility
compassionate hating heartily
full of fantastic visions

Blood in her arteries torments her
with the bliss of nightly steppes
Flames appease her thirst
Maiden
with widespread wings
she tears headlong into the cross
And kneeling
She flings with her whole might a stone
at injustice
and the whorish male laws
Resisting
every muddy soul
not surrendering to the sword

Possessed by genuineness
she loathes all humiliation
desperately devoted to bright light
she flees
into the flames of her fate

Blažena Vilemína
sister of tenacity
bride of purity
blazing rose

She wanders under Latin skies
and rears up

against scintillating rays of darkness
delivered to starving packs

Some day they'll call her
Guglielma Bohema
They'll dig out her bones
burn them in disgrace
and scatter her ashes
no one knows where

Even if

Even if the intrigues of minions and the fondling of torturers
joined to conspire together
and complete darkness surrounded me
nothing would turn away my steps
nothing in this world
which worships itself
and sins as if gone mad

Perjurers claim fidelity
the rich through gorging shed blood
judges mock justice
and insolence goes hand in hand with them

Embezzlers are raised
to ill-famed honors
which spread god-like through the land
and fawn up to the cross pierced through

No!
Cries every vein
recoiling in disgust
meanwhile a single one of my faithful
barefoot and poor
living on spring water and forest fruits
in tatters carries through the regions of night
a lampstand which quenches the body's hunger
and the soul's thirst

Bless by your death the light

Scarf around your neck Ludmila!
A pack of furious dogs
Broke into the September night
Desecrated the chapel
where the mother of the poor
ignited the Word

A dove fleeing towards a darkened sky
with a twig of tenderness
they choked
muddied vengeance in their blood
For holding out compassionate hands
wrath in the executioners' hearts

Flames of incendiaries
       not fires peacefully suffusing hearths
Idolaters of cruel trials
drunk with blasphemy-
       and she to dejected multitudes
       dealt out hunks of hope

Sword on your heart Václav!
They stained even the morning mass
While out of the scorched earth
he raised peace
and to his lips applied dew
the destroyers
       swore an oath on iron

Perusing his conscience through the night
he humbly entered
into Christ's silence
inclined towards the orphans and the poor
       while they
       full of frenzy
       sacrificed to death

Conscious of his land's lot

he wished to endow it with bread
        against hatred smoldering from inside
        which had infested ducal courts
Familiar with grief he invoked light
on all of God's creatures

He gave himself up
to sword and treason
which surrounded him in brotherly love
and cut

Bless these earthly strivings of mine
Ludmila
Václav
bless by your death the light
to which I am drawn

Fin Amor

It reeks of game in the banquet hall still
They would swallow darkness
Under their feet gnawed bones
and from overturned pewter flows blood
suddenly below the torches a clap of shoes
and a band of jugglers and jesters
gives a yell on command

Trumpeters stand up in the night
agape at exhausted tables
ears blocked against wailing pipers

On the couches fornicators
swoon
between the fool and the executioner
till numbness

But the roar itself is dying down now
starting to snore
on the wings of bats
Suddenly before midnight
out of the hush rises
the lucid lute under the fingers of Reinmar
stroking her nape

She invokes the most faithful Morning Star
And the swan singing till death
She confesses her love
to the spring dawn
overflowing with greenery
and the rain
in which the royal harps were rekindled

Lips likened to a rose
She alone knows it
and that stranger

whenever his eyes burn hers
and his thrilling song
gives a quick sharp bite to her soul
which wanders with the mute moon
through the voiceless sky

The very stones joined hands in prayer

Hurled down boulders
oppress the earth's breast
Hunger in human wastelands
Even the beast's throats tighten with anguish
whenever the lowery sky bursts
and the land is nailed to the cross

Plague in the downpours
With brutal voices
the wretched bang
on warm windows

Unrecognized in rags of poverty
she stands in front of God amid complaining crowds
The neighbor was created
to receive mercy
where wheat flutters
and warm waters wash wounds

She does penance for daily horrors
as if they clung to her hands
and she could not ward them off
except with her heart

Nightingales pause and listen to the song
of Brother Francis ardently praising the rain
and the sun a gerbera in his mouth
Wolf and deer at his feet
The landscape bathed in azure
is like the treasure chest of the Czech Lands

The very stones join their hands in prayer
and their flames
from the cruel heathen darkness
leap up to heaven

Consecration

One last fond look
at the royal candelabras which turned
the pages of the Psalter
and in the silence hewn in the heart
one rear view glance
at the unstained days
of which not a word shall pass her lips

What's left is to say good-bye to the prayer stool
smooth down the flashy furs
on the relinquished bed
extinguish the jewels
before the walk to the most intense of lights

Humiliation wove her bridal gown by night
Un-humiliated
she dons on its brightness
her hair flowing round her shoulders
like a stream of flaming torches
Her face
sweetness itself
Her eyes a perianth
Pride on her forehead
Sunrise on her lips
More elegant than a night lotus
Descended from a lineage of songs and wellsprings
in the depth of which rings shine

How much darkness and death flowed
on the waters under Judith bridge
miseries that could not be heard
on the royal road
and were destined to sink
under the indifference of celestial gems

Her mother's gentleness clasps her inwardly
even as her father's defiance pulses in her blood
and straightens her spine

-Konstancie
brother Václav Kunhuta
princes of the land deign to look
at the enlightened humility
the soil she walks on
simple and surrendered

She summoned herself
as she meandered out of idle talk
and resolved to lift up the downtrodden cross
pledging herself to sacrifice
and to the mission sent by God
that her speech might resound forthright
through the realms of darkness

The flames of shorn locks
descend onto the cathedral pavement
bewailed in their fall
And a black scarf
veils her bare head

She lays aside her splendid worldly garment
and the gold delicate gem-studded sash
In stead
rough gray serge
and a tough rope
grip her body
She slips her bare feet
into wooden sandals
kneeling in front of the Crucified

Together with her
seven noble Czech maidens

No ! Let no lamentations
tremble under the slender windows
Let joy burst into song and color
Sun-like monstrance announce
the resurrection of the desolate land

breathing again through grasses and pines
with ankles washed
by gentle clear transparent waters

Poverty - the greatest of riches
She overflows with all things
She is free

Lamp of hope

By the hospital dispensary
fog infested fellows
shuffle from early dawn
Like a rumble of storm clouds
cripples' canes hit the pavement

Fever devours the lungs of the wretches
Clad in despair
Mangy dogs by their feet
Sunk in mud without help
Death has marked them
tearing all light from their faces

Miserable Speechless
Suffering In travail
Humiliated On their knees
Erring From night to night
Bleeding Rotting away

It is written:
        Foxes have lairs
        birds of the air nests
        but the son of man has
        nowhere to lay his head

Even to blood obsessed rapists
drunken arsonists
murderers' whores
prowlers working intrigues and evil
Good must be done !
What are we if not grass seeds
in mercy grown on plains or gutters ?
What are we but blind rain smoldering in the soil ?

But heaven orders:
tear the bottomless darkness asunder
clear the muddy waters
do not shrink from the hideous ones

give your hand to the infected ones

Through action undo sinful indifference
In the inhospitable wasteland
shelter the chaotic crowds
Open hospitals
Give bread to the disgraced
offer drink of sage tea
and cleanse the wounds of the soul
in the seven- sorrowed land

Rather than a proud queen of foreigners
be a refuge of light
to your own
never weary
a lamp of hope

Reconciliation

Wretchedness of the Slavnikovs
sticks to the parchment
and oozes through scraps of prayers

Nothing will cleanse blood-slugging rain
not even sacrificing to fire

Repentance?
It will not stone to death its own guilt
heritage of an un-merciful clan
possessed at the dawn of its homeland
by hunger for power.

Extinguish lawlessness through blood ?

Meanwhile the light loving land
abounds with wisdom of forests
and through the lute of wheat fields flows
into the silent sky
beyond the horizon of stars

The king credulous minion of nebulous skies
invites minstrels to revels in the night
where for depths of pleasure
and wings of delirium
he would give his scepter

At midnight still he orders
his flushed companions
to set out towards Kamyk castle
where pheasants rise like kindling
and deer glide into the twilight glades
There the alluring moon lies naked on the waves
till dawn spreads open the draperies of mists
Over the flaxen river glen

But no peace is granted to these regions
who could shine

and lay their diadems into treasure chests
guarded by mountain forts and wide water courses
if but arsonists did not pull them down into the abyss

Blood flares up again
for foreigners to appease
brother against brother rises up to the death
more savage than wild beasts

Only after they have split the land in two
and proclaimed the son ruler over his father
above the smoldering cities
near the tomb of the queen
whose heart was pierced by discord
the king appeals to his own truth

-He who lifts up treason
and joins with it
will be himself one day betrayed

Anežka sends out
a dove of words
towards both armies
let king and prince consider their hatreds
and hear reconciliation in their hearts

In the convent hall the crown rests
on Václav's head
Like autumn leaves from an oak
anger cruelty and unrelenting vengeance fall away
all sides awash in light
kindled for the sake of her brethren
and her downtrodden land
by sister Anežka

The exiles

Spy after spy collects in the countryside
Each night a draught from somewhere
and mothers' hearts tightened with sudden horror
reach for the cradle in their sleep

They suspect what others do not hear
The orphaned land turns towards them
its grasses wailing
under the hoofs of approaching herds

Somewhere in darkness the steppes opened
up to the raven filled sky
Under it grandsons of Gingiskan are looting
torches gallop
Flares of weeping villages They plunder monasteries
pouring bloody chalices down their throats
From the south towards midnight
the sons of the chosen son
who do not spare even the throats of children
overflow rye fields and meadows

But from lairs and mountain caves
like hounded beasts
the exiles keep their watch
for the monstrance of God's bread

Children of Death

Bells will not stop ringing
        In the silence of terror
Under a canopy of birches
rising up in the translucent blue
        Downpours crisscross the sky
In the footprints of birds
Dawn
        From torn shoes
        Bleed little pink heels
Dressed in silk
Shining with cleanliness
In black rotting rags
        They trudge through mud
Radiating health and light
        Pierced through with fevers
Younglings of serene plains
        Over rock chasms
Cheering festive throats
        Do not utter a sound
Milk and bread
and spring water
        Weak with hunger
        Dark with thirst
On fire with sacred songs
        They weep

Towards the candelabras of the holy grave
cast down in mud
a road strewn with roses
Its dust sprinkled with holy water

With Holy Communion they open the heavens
clouds of which organ sounds tear apart
Swords of condescending leaders
bless the humble procession

Above the waters the cross lifts high its bloody nails
and the children
wandering phantoms of an expanding world
fall into death

Mother of Seven Sorrows

Countless times has the land
heard its streams and torrents moan
as swords of intruders washed their blood in them
and forces of darkness broke encampments
on the midnight shores
Linden trees glowing with honey even towering oaks
countless times burned to the roots and wells
blocked with human bodies polluted the soil

The land sealed with seven sorrows
can't even sigh over her plundered pines
or lift up orphaned falcons to the rain
or against raging elements thrust her hands
so as to protect her native ores and jewels
still blazing on the borders of her plains

They exterminated birds nests before her eyes
knocked down larks from the skies and reduced to dust
wings that used to blaze like flames

So a tomb like silence spread and anguish gusts from calamities
to which sparrows bees and butterflies fall in sacrifice
while rotting carrion litters the reddened horizon

And forever and ever hunger devours A lunacy
wastelands where the wretched reach
towards the foul scraps from the gluttony of the mighty
the thirsty drag themselves on their knees towards puddles
to quench their bodies darkness

Crowds rush headlong into plague burials
alive only in God
Moldering lungs beg for air
From wombs of mothers newborn float away to nothingness
Not even tears are heard in this dull terror
and nowhere even a shred of coming daybreak
Opulence's misery maid of death

The land's powerless heart stiffens with pain
as she sees recruiter hatred marching through the countryside
calling under her flag hordes with empty stomachs
driving them to revenge with blood thick wine
late into the night then abandoning them to their fate
these lives whose Christian name at birth had been hope

The word is torn from their lips and thrown to the dogs
Infected ones blame others   Each scab a treason
If only in the mouth !
        They spit in the center of the heart
If only silence !
        But these perverters of speech
plot against the very life of luminous Czech
to which immaterial air gave wings
to abate gales
forged in pure fire
akin to water lutes

The language
scrambles from under a cliff and sprouts from the soil
lovely
with a pure graceful complexion

Anger's sword of justice hardened within
Subject to no verdicts she drinks from her own sources
she will not stand as witness to blessings of vileness
Mother tongue
inflorescence most tenacious
star studded jewel case
tabernacle
poetry's firmament
shield

Not a single song drifts through the universe of clouds
not one grass moves in the plains
Even the rains stopped for which the fields thirst
and not a tread of light comes to greet
a dawn collapsed on the doorstep

To the bottom of the abyss she the eagle has fallen
daughter of liberty blood of my blood and yours
The evening dew alone washes out her wounds
a sound rings out in death tolls and in dumps
from the Hercyn forests to the plains of Polabí
from clouds over Krušné Mountains to the Moravian waters
wherever freedom walks on its beggar's stick

Sorrow of sorrows woe of woes horror of horrors
as she accompanies her daughters and sons
into the fog of exile she supports their cross
and stands by them in despair only through prayer

Homeland of outcasts death hounds and lies
humiliated by darkness
but homeland still
of everlasting peace
and Czech truth

A hundred hearts began to beat

A hundred hearts began to beat against dark bell metal
over the town for the dead And in the death tolls of crows
orphans' laments as many as burned out grasses
Churches gape open   From the Moravian field
howls the myrmidons' roar as they tear
the royal robes to rags and drag along the naked body
through mud and stones into the throat of ignominy
Berthold Schenk from Murderberg death bearer from Emberg
trusts out his palm and behind him Czech spite
those packs from behind lustful executioners
Rats and slander creeping everywhere
fanfares of slippery treasons Thanksgiving rumbles
for the love of intruders and the glory of looting

What to them are bars darkness hunger plague in the kingless land
collapsed into the paws of tyrants !
They do not see the myrmidons they do not hear the prince
nor the land that the world proclaimed anathema
and so many Pontius Pilates surrendered to foreign rabble
Carts loaded with carrion creak through the nights
and blackened heads drum into the soil
Crowds of wretches fling themselves hungrily
on bones together with the beasts and gnaw the bark of trees

Whole villages died out tabernacles were plundered
crown jewels dishonored   the queen
and her son languish in the towers of Zitava
And the holy guardian chokes on silver
As decreed in the treaty of the protectors
let the whole land a beggar be silent on her knees!
And our blood is to honor these Brandenburg dogs

Slender Flame

Slender flame
      flashing up from a maiden's hands
      you cut down adversity
Light holder
      with your rays you tame darkness
      persistent as Marah's bitter waters
Morning Star
      Whenever breath itself is lacking
      and earth caves in
      you stop horrified and buttress
      luminous
      the despair of waters and the abandon of mouths
Offspring of royal stock
      You float above the Czech Land with the rain
      and quench her feverish thirst
Healer of wounds
      You bend over
      lay on bandages
      lead the lost home
      with your word heal the soul
      and remove all malignancy
Counselor of rulers
      You join the hands of straying men
      cleansing hatred from their hearts
      so as to protect the skies
      from foreign predators
Benefactress
      taking under your wings
      all God's creatures
      humans, beasts of the fields, plants in the ditches
Confessor of poverty
      you cling to her like to a sister
      and cast off all jewels
Venerator of humility
      which sets a diadem in your hair
      you reject all violence

Quiet modesty
Consecrated to the bleeding star
Kind-hearted servant
       following Christ
       so nothing can obstruct good deeds
       which you harvest like ripe apples
       and distribute to the poor

Woman
       in purity abounding
       morning light
Gentle mother
       graciously compassionate
Slender flame

She finds God

She finds God
wherever she walks
Friend of kings as well as of the poor
forgiving humankind
for even ugliness and evil
come out of the will of God

She lays a balm on wounds
which cannot close over
To accusing mouths she offers water
whose spring she calls forth
from under the stones

Hungry herself
she bars the way to hunger

Anguished
she consoles the miserable
whose hearts stumble in the dark
She serves the light that visits her
in hours of need

Lifting up the lost
taking away suffering
she despises the mantle of worldly glory
confesses purity
subject to nothing
except the truth of the word that guides her
unthreatened
over impassable roads, mud and rocks
into the freedom of Scriptures

First letter Of Claire on poverty

To the waters of Bohemia
beyond mountain borders
over wild primeval forests
clouds carry this letter to my sister
She chose most holy poverty
while she could have espoused
honors and power!
She set aside the royal crown
while she could have adorned herself with pearls
O time distorting moon
you spread shadows in our way
so as to turn our steps away
from disdaining imperial estates
yet poverty of the mortal body
is but riches of the soul
Light giving perianth!
Poor daisy dear to my heart
above all worldly glory

Second letter about Christ

Last of all men
despised
both by the mighty and the masses
more wretched than a hounded beast
hated
cursed by his own
spied on by the filthiest of filthy minded
betrayed for a serpent's stone
stained with saliva
snubbed
bleeding
delivered to mockery
destitute hungry
abandoned in his wounds
imprisoned by rage
denounced as one of the stigmatized race
delivered to death by the unsatisfied
crucified

First among all
honored
by the poor and the pure hearted
stronger than elemental powers
beloved
Invoked in the heart
accompanied by songs
embraced through nights and days
bright
acclaimed with roses
healed
glorified through our humility
bountiful fulfilled
throngs of believers at his feet
free through love
shuttering prisons

stepping into life towards those who thirst
risen from the dead

Third letter about pride of the powerful

Even if up to heaven rose
their pride
its head touching the clouds
in the end it will be hurled down like dregs

They are deluded the kings of this world
who let mouths be shut closed
and who against the words of truth muster darkness
They bring upon themselves the anger
of downtrodden lands and waters
from which the uninvited drink

From everywhere a deep brilliance wells up
driving away intrigues of perjurers

With our last breath
let us stand up against them-
Christian judgment

Fourth letter about the defiant birch tree

From the silence where we live like happy flower children
my letters leave
but rarely
for messengers are scarce
and hundreds of dangers threaten the roads

Barefoot near springs of water
amidst songs in high grass
we rejoice in the Lord's gifts
for there is not a day
but from our hands
a remedy arises
the garden is cared for
and Christ's dwelling is adorned

You persevere in holy service in your native land
in spite all obstacles
as if you were not a frail woman
but a birch tree defying
hurricanes, lightning and floods

Know
that your name will be
in the book of life.

Death of Agnes of Bohemia

Suddenly darkness close to the heart
The March earth felt chilled to the bone

In front of the dispensary at prayers hunger
the downtrodden words of beggars
rear up before the monastery walls
where a pure spring is hidden

By the simple bed
behind her head silence is waiting
Now there remains only to turn to the sisters
with a last kind word mollify their weeping
and take unto herself their pain
even at this moment.

Her father in whose heart tenderness and sword were welded
brother Vaclav to whom she was dearer than anything on earth
even her beloved nephews
from blood and humiliation as well as prison bars
imposed on them by verdicts of foreigners
have come to her

Daisies lighten the pillow under her head
All the kindness
which she gave to the end
returns to her
wiping beads from her brow
The healed wash her burning lips
and thirst which she quenched in her neighbor
gives her to drink

Pure of soul
she entrusts the wretched to the order of love
One last time she blesses her humiliated homeland
and the sky above it
that its yoke and dark tolls might be lifted
and light arise over the royal land

Her mother Konstancie strokes her hair
and with the sign of the cross upon her forehead
prepares her for the journey of light

Death
the closest of her sisters
cancelled agony in her body

Over her face settled
a grace-filled peace

End notes

Notes accompanying individual poems are drawn from historical and belletristic sources about the life and achievements of Agnes of Bohemia.

(Notes in parentheses are added by the translator jmk)

Gentleness nestled in her

Anežka was born on January 20, 1208 in Prague, probably at Vyšehrad. Daughter of King Přemysl Otakar I and Konstancie of Hungary, she was given from her earliest days a high degree of education. She spent three years, with her sister Anna, and their aunt Hedwig, in the Cistercian monastery of Třebonice. After that she spent a year in a Premonstratien monastery, two years in Prague and at the age of nine, she was sent for five years to Vienna.

She spoke so patiently to the flowers of the fields

Legends as well as various historical works, depict Anežka as a sensitive, lyrical, young woman, whose ralationship to nature, people, the world, was steeped in real Franciscan love, gentleness and deep feelings of devotion. At the same time, in all the important moments of her life, she showed herself a woman of action, unwavering decisions and firm stance, a blessed inheritance of the Premyslid, unbreakable will. (*verbasca, from verbascum austriacum, a plant resembling the lupinus or delphinium, with tall stalks covered with yellow, rose like flowers with bright orange centers. It is an endangered species from the Carpathian Tatras, homeland of the poet. It speaks of the poet's knowledge and love of nature. jmk)

O Mother Tongue

It is clear Anežka spoke several languages— undoubtedly German and Latin since it is known she listened to troubadour songs and wrote letters in both of these. Her affinity for her mother tongue, however, did not weaken, even during her long stays abroad, where she let everyone know she was a Czech princess from the Premyslid family.

In her heart anguished darkness

In 1217 at the age of nine, Anežka was sent to the court of Vienna where she was to become engaged to Henry VII, the son of the German emperor. But in 1222 she returned to Prague. Henri VII married instead Margaret of Austria, whom he divorced a few years later. In 1231 he asked for Anežka's hand, but was refused along with the emperor himself and the King of England, who were all her suitors. Anežka's resolve to enter religious life was supported by the pope, Gregory IX.

Your name Konstancie

Anežka's mother, Konstancie, came from Hungary. She was the daughter of King Bela III. In 1199 she became the second wife of King Přemysl Otakar I. She was known for her deep piety and she clearly had a considerable influence on the education of her children, especially her daughters: Judita-Jitka, Anna, Anežka and Blažena-Vilemina. Towards the end of her life she joined the cistercian monastery of Tišnov, in Moravia. She died in 1240. Her sister was Queen Elisabeth of Hungary, later canonized.

Whenever fire

Anežka's younger sister, Blažena Vilemína, was born in 1210. She traveled to Italy, where she co-founded a religious group, which fought for equal rights for women in the Catholic Church. She was known as Gugliema Bohema. She died in Milan in 1281. Twenty years after her death, her remains were burnt and scattered.

Even if

Many documents witness to the fact that Anežka knew how to pursue her goals in an uncompromising fashion, and that she therefore collided, in particular, with some Church authorities in Prague. However, the gift of a critical mind was linked in her with a rare purity of faith. She did not join the order and did not enter the convent, just to distance herself from worldly life, but rather, so that her influence might be freer and more effective.

Bless by your death the light

The cult of Ludmila and her grandson Václav began already in the lifetime of Anežka. Following the early popular legends, we find at the end of the first millenium, Kristian's Chronicle in Latin about the life and death of St. Václav and St. Ludmila. Later, this period of Czech history is described by Kosmas, a Canon of the Prague Chapter. The composition of the chorale *Sv. Václave* can be put to the Twelveth century. (Václav, Ludmila and Anežka are three of the main patron saints of the Czech Lands. Václav, the Wenceslas of the English carol, a good and peaceful ruler of the Tenth century, was assassinated on his way to early mass, by henchmen of his pagan brother Boleslav. Václav's grandmother Ludmila, one of the first Czech Christians, known for her goodness to the poor, was choked to death with her own veil on the orders of her daughter-in-law, Drahomira. Jmk)

Fin Amor

At the royal court of Anežka's brother Václav, lived many troubadours, among them also Reinmar von Zweter. They were an outstanding part of cultural life in the Czech Lands.

The very stones joined hands in prayer

Anežka's joining of the Order of the Poor Clares was the result of long meditations on genuine religious and life experiences. Her decision was most certainly influenced by her family environment and her education. She was above all attracted by the ideas of St. Francis about humble service to God in total poverty, as a source of freedom, and about love of neighbor as demonstrated in acts of mercy and humanity. The example of Chiara Scifi, St. Clare, who left behind the riches of the world and embraced poverty in 1212, was another factor, which shaped Anežka's life's calling and destiny.

Consecration

In 1234, Anežka, age 26, enters the convent, following a ceremony at St. Francis Church, and becomes a simple sister of the order of Poor Clares. Seven young noble Czech ladies enter with her. Anežka brings to the convent and the hospital for the poor her dowry, later increased through the gifts of her brother King Václav I, her mother Konstancie and the contributions of Czech lords. (Judith Bridge was the first bridge over the Vltava, built before and in the same place as the Charles bridge, built in the fourteenth century and still there today. It was at the start of the "royal road," which lead up from the old town to the castle. jmk)

Lamp of hope

Following the example of her cousin Elisabeth, Anežka founded near St. Francis Convent a hospital for the poor. Later she started the order of Crusaders of the Red Star "for temporal as well as spiritual needs." Besides her religious duties, she worked tirelessly both in the convent and in the hospital, cleaning and heating the sisters' cells, doing laundry, mending clothes, cooking both for the convent and the hospital, washing the dishes and nursing the sick.

Reconciliation

King Václav I, a lover of tournaments, courtly entertainments, and troubadour songs, a frequent participant at hunts and banquets, spent a great deal of time at his various castles and, towards the end of his reign, became less and less interested in the management of the affairs of state and the securing of power. In 1248 a group of Czech lords elected in Prague the "Younger King," Václav's son, Přemysl Otakar. Václav was forced to set out against Prague. In 1249 he put down the rebellion, with the help of Austrian and Hungarian armies, and condemned several of its participants to death. Anežka is credited with settling the dispute between the relatives. In the hall she reconciled father and son. The bishops of Prague and of Olomouc set on Václav's head the Czech crown. The son Přemysl Otakar was given the rule of Moravia. (Together Czechy, also called Bohemia, and Moravia make up the Czech Lands or the Lands of the Czech Crown. jmk)

The Exiles

In 1241 Moravia was overrun by Tatars. Europe as a whole was then threatened by about half a million soldiers from the Eastern steppes, highly trained in "surprise warfare," consisting of nightly moves on super fast horses and sudden surprise attacks. The army of King Vaclav I stood up against them. After the encounter at Olomouc, the army, lead by Gingiskan's grandson Batue, abandoned the conquest of the land and returned home. (This victory without a fight, possibly due to a sudden plague, is commemorated to this day, by a yearly pilgrimage to the Marian Shrine on the Holy Hill near Olomouc. A large painting shows Mary blessing all, as the armies pack up and go home. jmk)

Children of Death

The thirteenth century saw the formation of the Children's Crusades, which were supposed to free Christ's tomb in the Holy Land. The majority of children, which included children from the Czech Lands, perished either from exhaustion or sickness during these expeditions. Often they were killed or captured and sold into slavery. Saint Francis opposed these expeditions from the depth of his heart.

Mother of Seven Sorrows

Towards the end of her life, after the tragic death of Premysl Otakar II, hard times came on the kingdom and its people. Anežka worked tirelessly to lighten as much as possible the lot of the poor and the sick.

A hundred hearts began to beat

Between 1278 and 1282, after the death of Přemysl Otakar II, the Czech lands went through the so-called "king-less" period. The eight year old prince Václav and his mother, queen Kunhuta, were imprisoned in various places, among them Žitava Castle. Otto Brandenburg and after him Bishop Eberhard impoverished and ill-treated the land, which at the time was tried by famine, plague, natural disasters and crop failures. Half a million people died in the Czech lands during that period. Only a year after Anežka's death, was Prince Václav able to return, sit on the throne and assume leadership of the country.

Slender Flame

The actions of Anežka Česká were pervaded by virtues coming from her deeply lived Christian faith. Linking religious devotion with self-sacrificing activity, Anežka entered Czech history as a protector of true humanity.

She finds God

The exemplary life of Anežka, a life consecrated and completely given to God's truth and humanity, led to the fact that from ancient times, the Czech people wished and prayed for her canonization.

The four letters of St Claire to Agnes of Bohemia

The Four Letters in Latin, were sent by St. Claire, founder of the Order of the Poor Clares, from the convent of San Damiano Italy, to Agnes of Bohemia, witness to Anežka's fruitful relationship with the very heart of the Franciscan movement. The letters sent by Anežka to Claire were not preserved. Besides her correspondence with Claire, Anežka sent twenty two letters to the Vatican, to Pope Gregory IX, who thought very highly of her, supported her endeavors and gave her good advice.

Death of Agnes of Bohemia

Anežka died on March 2, 1282 after 9 p. m. in the convent of St. Francis, at a time when her country was under the occupation of foreign armies. She was seventy-four years old and was buried in the Chapel of Our Lady. The life and the merciful acts of Anežka Česká were never forgotten. They are kept in the memory of the Czech people to this day.

Postlude by Maria Nemcova Banerjee
Professor of Russian and Comparative Literature
Smith College

History rarely opens up to the miraculous, perhaps least of all in the Czech lands. And yet, during the dark centuries of historical dispossession, threatened with the extinction of their high culture and their beloved language, the Czech people clung to the legends and prophecies of national resurrection. In 1918, the advent of national independence brought great joy and pride to a nation renewed. But in the rear view mirror of the late twentieth century the two decades of the First Republic, exuberantly creative and impressive in their social and political achievements, could appear like a brief idyll framed by the blood-soaked fields of Flanders and the betrayal at Munich.

On the small stage of ancient Bohemia, the deadly logic of European history was revealed in the nightmarish form of Nazism and Communism. For the Czechs who lived through those years—1918 followed by 1938 and 1948—
the historical script was marked by a pattern of repetition alternating with brief episodes of false renewal. The last of these, known as the Prague Spring of 1968, confirmed the suspicion of many that the secular time of Communism had gone dead in its track. After an enforced "normalization," the regime lingered on for twenty more years as the spirit of the land settled into a troubled sleep.

Then, unexpectedly, the spell of evil historical rhyming was broken in 1989. During that singular year, as those who lived it remember, every significant date on the Czech national calendar would give rise to a spontaneous popular demonstration followed by instant police repression. On November 12, 1989, the long delayed canonization of Agnes of Bohemia was proclaimed by a Slavic Pope and true to the prophecy, "a great marvel happened in the land." Exactly a week later, the people rattled their keys on St. Vaclav's Square and two of the leaders of what became known as the Velvet Revolution addressed them from the balcony. Standing side by side with Vaclav Havel, the heir of the humanist tradition of the First Republic, the Catholic priest Vaclav Maly was a

51

messenger from the submerged soul of Czech mysticism, signifying the spiritual meaning of the occasion, as if Agnes the Premyslid, daughter and sister of Czech Kings, had stepped out of her thirteenth century niche to shed the grace of her charity on the parched land, and turn the hope of civic renewal into a moment of redemption.

Jaromir Horec's poetic cycle, *Agnes of Bohemia*, from which verses were read on the Czech television on November 27, 1989, weaves together legend and history in shades of light and darkness. The dramatic story of the saint's life, commanded by the imperative of renunciation and service, is presented in counterpoint with running allusions to the morally tarnished atmosphere of the terminal decade of Czech Communism when the poem was written. The plain narrative line is adorned by the inclusion of lyrical poems in the form of invocation, litany and epistle, shining like gems among the smaller grains of a rosary. To recreate the medieval mood of prayerful concentration, Horec uses irregular, short-lined stanzas that dispense with the end rhyme, relying on euphony and anaphoric repetition for its subtle, subdued rhythm. In deploying the elevated lexicon and the arcane phrasing of liturgical diction, Horec is making an implied statement and a plea in favor of the lost dignity of Czech language, which had been coarsened by a phony proletarianization.

The first two poems in the sequence of twenty-six, "Gentleness nestled in her" and "She spoke so patiently to the flowers of the fields," define the Franciscan ideal of humble service that shaped Agnes' monastic vocation. Helped by her deep understanding of Franciscan spirituality, Jana Moravkova Kiely's English translation achieves a near perfect transparency for the Czech text, where the stately pace of heraldic description vies with the fervor of a spoken voice.

In the third poem, "O Mother Tongue," the language of prayer merges imperceptibly with the mystical eroticism of the language of *cortesia*. It ends on the untranslatable Czech word *Milost*, left in the original by the translator who adds three English words—Grace, Loveliness, Compassion-- to explicate its multilayered meaning. In the last line of the final poem of the series, "Death of Agnes of

Bohemia" the same semantic root of the word *milost* returns as the adjective *milostny*, which carries a distinct erotic connotation in modern Czech usage. The translation renders it as "a grace-filled peace." That choice is wholly appropriate for the event it describes, death as a solemn passage from the temporal to the eternal. Agnes experienced death in the spirit of St. Francis, evoked by the preceding two lines: "Death/ the closest of her sisters/ cancelled agony in her body."

As I reread the poem in praise of Agnes' Czech mother tongue, I overhear in it an echo of Dante's Valley of the Negligent Princes in Purgatorio VII, where the poet-pilgrim spends his first night on the mountain in a shelter hollowed in the austere stone, but richly adorned with precious gems of all colors. Dante's companions, the kings atoning for the vanity and recklessness of their worldly life, are Agnes' kinsmen—her father Premysl Otakar I and her brother Vaclav, whose violent discord she helped reconcile to secure peace in her native land. hat dramatic moment in the legend of her life is depicted in the poem "Reconcilation."

The Dantean resonance in a poem about the Czech language may not be deliberate, but it pulls together the spiritual and national dimensions of Agnes' life. That same strain of mystical patritotism is present in the loving evocation of the topography of Agnes' native city, with the "royal river that God unfurled at the feet of Prague," a line that clearly alludes to the medieval topos of the river as Divine Grace. It was on the shores of the Vltava that Agnes built a hospital for the poor, where she officiated by assuming the most arduous physical tasks usually reserved for the lowliest servants. The building, as Jana Moravkova Kiely notes in her introduction, was still in use in 1945, when she and I would walk past it as schoolgirls.

"Lamp of Hope," with its vivid account of the plague stricken poor to whom Agnes ministered, also serves as a transition to the sequence of dark poems placed in the middle of the cycle. The theme of fratricidal war, following on the heels of usurpation and betrayal finds expression in four poems of lamentation: "The exiles," "Children of Death," "Mother of Seven Sorrow ," "A Hundred Hearts." The translator admits that these poems about the historical calamities unleashed by the few on the many, with their harvest of devastating hatred, gave her most trouble. Still, she did well by them, using harsh alliterations of grating sounds and sibilants to capture the feel of the Czech original.

The central metaphor of the flame, already announced in "Lamp of Hope" where it flickers with a steady light of Agnes' disciplined charity, finds it fullest expression in the litany "Slender Flame." Here the diction rises to prayer, as if in atonement for the dark poems that preceded it. The poem marks the passage of Agnes' life in history into her eternal glory as a future saint and legendary protectress of the Czech people. I note that Horec's cycle includes a poem of homage to Agnes' less fortunate sister Vilemina, who entered Church history as Gugliema Bohema. Entangled in the politics of thirteenth century Italy, she was declared a heretic and her body was burnt after her death, its ashes scattered. In "Whenever fire" Horec pays tribute to her passionate love of justice. Vilemina's fierce flame, stoked to conflagration by an intransigent commitment to the truth, stands in sharp contrast to Agnes' delicately tender tongue of flame, a metaphor for her spirit that comforts and warms us even as it lights the way. Vilemina, a soul of air and fire, represents that other pole of Czech religious history, revered in the figure of Jan Hus and in the civic martyr Jan Palach.

The four poems based on the letters of St. Claire to Agnes, placed immediately before the cycle closes with Agnes' death, encapsulate the spiritual core of the cycle. While the correspondence between the two women is historically true, Agnes' letters have been lost, leaving us with a void that can only be filled if we intuit her voice from the voice of the older saint. The mystery of the absent voice is further heightened by the strange coincidence of the disappearance of Agnes' body, which made the process of canonization more problematic. In the decisive move made by John Paul II, St. Claire's letters were cited as evidence. Thus, St. Claire's words, offered in testimony to Agnes' holiness, dramatize the Biblical mystery of the Word becoming flesh. Further, in the vivid imagery of Horec's four poems, the original prose of the letters has been transformed into a defining verbal emblem of Agnes' saintliness.

ABOUT THE AUTHOR

Jaromír Hořec was born on December 18, 1921 in Chust, in Sub-Carpathian Ruthenia, which in 1919, at the treaty of Versailles, had voted to become part of the newly formed Czechoslovak Republic with an enlightened, freely elected government led by the humanist philosopher, Tomas Garrigue Masaryk.

During World War I, Hořec's father had fought with the famed foreign legions in Russia, which became the founding elements of the new Czechoslovak army. He was a forest ranger. Forest rangers had been from the beginning of time immemorial supervisors and protectors of the ecosystem of the treasured primeval border forests. Taking care of trees as well as wounded animals, they could be called the first environmentalists. Thus from his childhood, Jaromír Hořec developed a great love and respect for nature as well as for a just, enlightened, democratic, national leadership. In 1938, after the disaster of Munich, Czechoslovakia was invaded and broken up into several parts by Hitler. Throughout the Nazi occupation of Czechoslovakia, Jaromír Hořec was active in the underground anti-Nazi youth movement. After World War II, Sub-Carpathian Ruthenia was not returned to Czechoslovakia but was annexed by Stalin to the Soviet Union. Thus Hořec, living in Prague, became an expatriate in his own country. In 1945, he was the founder of Mladá Fronta. In 1950, after the Communist take over he was forced to resign.

He studied Czech literature at Charles University in Prague and obtained his doctorate in 1954. From 1965, during the period known as Prague Spring, he worked as assistant professor of sociology and editor of the review UK at Charles University. In 1969, after the Soviet invasion, he was forced to resign these posts. Though he was a prolific poet, he was not allowed to publish for two periods of twenty years each: 1948-1966 and 1969-1989.

In 1977, he signed Charter 77 and in 1979 he founded the Czech underground press Ceska Expedice for which he was imprisoned in 1981. The prison experience, as well as memories of the 1968 Soviet invasion, inspired his poems for *Dílna Holderinova* (*The Workshop of Friedrich Holderlin*). *Pozdvihovani Slov* (*The Raising of Words*) is based on his involvement with Charter 77. From the events of August 1968, the Soviet invasion, came *Soundní Den (Doom's Day.)* His many works of poetry, including *Anežka Česká,* and *Chléb Na Stole,* as well as many other publications, such as *Why I Am Not a Communist* and *Sub-Carpathian Ruthenia-an Unknown land* have been coming out only since 1989.

Another one of his remarkable activities has been in the area of jazz music for which he composed lyrics particularly during the period of the Prague Spring.

He serves as president of The Friends of Sub-Carpathian Ruthenia as well as vice president of the Masaryk Democratic Action Committee. He was long time editor of its review, ČAS.

Hořec describes his own thought processes which span over more than three quarters of a century, from the catastrophes of World War II, across the tragic darkness of the Communist era, to the complicated political reality of present day, as leading him back to the work and legacy of Tomas Masaryk, particularly his Christian humanism and his teachings on freedom and democracy.

Lumír Šindelář

Lumír Šindelář was born on January 15, 1925 in Rejdice u Jablonce nad Nisou, a region of Bohemia known for centuries for its artistic treatment of glass. (See Harvard University Glass Flowers collection.) From 1945-1951, he studied painting at AVU in Prague.

He has brought his original and inovative spirit to many different media. He is a painter, engraver, sculptor, creator of commemorative medals, stamps and an ex-libris, book illustrator and engraver on glass. He is the author of many frescoes and mosaics, as well as monumental sculptures and reliefs, such as the notable collection in the church of St. Peter and Paul at Vyšehrad, and the painted wood relief of the cross in the church of Our Lady of Emmaus in Prague.

His medals commemorate historical places and events, such as Terezin in 1972, In memoriam for Terezin's Children 1987, the Czech Catholic Caritas, and for the Ecumenical Translation of Scriptures in 1988. Others are remarkable portraits *en face* surrounded by symbolic elements. These include: a self-portait, Jan Hus, Dante Alighieri, Michelangelo, Gregor Mendel, R.J.Jeffers, F. Rabelais, Cervantes, Vaclav Hollar, Antonin Dvorak, Vincent van Gogh, Rembrandt, Goya, Sigmund Freud, and Rainer Maria Rilke, to name just a few.

Lumír Šindelář has often been called a renaissance man. He himself however explains the scope of his artistic achievements by saying he needed to feed his family while refusing to serve ideologies and -isms. Except for the period of the Prague Spring and then again after 1989, he was unable to get any official commission and was excluded from all official artists groups.

His son of the same name is now a well-known landscape architect for the city of Prague.

ABOUT THE TRANSLATOR

Jana Morávková Kiely was born in Prague in 1937. Her father was a lawyer, serving as cultural attaché with the Czechoslovak diplomatic mission in Paris. Her mother was the youngest daughter of František Udržal, minister of national defense and prime minister during the First Czechoslovak Republic.
After Hitler's brutal annexation of their country, Jana and her family survived World War II on their ancestral farms, deep in the Bohemian countryside. In 1948, following the Communist takeover of Czechoslovakia, Jana had to go into exile with her parents and sister Liba, (Libuše Paukertová Lehárová). She attended the French Lycée in Casablanca Morrocco and got her undergraduate degree in Biology from the Sorbonne, Paris.
In 1958 she came to Harvard University to pursue a PhD in Genetics. From 1964-75 she taught Biology at Newton College of the Sacred Heart (later merged with Boston College.) In 1979, she obtained a Master's in Theological Studies from Harvard Divinity School. From 1981 to 94, she was director of religious education

at St Paul Church in Cambridge. In 1982-83, she taught at the University of Sichuan in Chengdu, China. From 1994-98, she was director of development for the Oblates of the Virgin Mary at St Clement's Shrine in Boston. From 1973-99 she was Co-Master of Adams House with her husband Robert Kiely, Loker professor of English Literature and Master of Adams House at Harvard University. The Kielys have four children and eight grandchildren.

ACKNOWLEDGEMENTS

So many friends encouraged me over the years I can mention only a few. To begin with I wish to remember Daria Donnelly who first took this work seriously and Catherine Morrissey who gave it her blessing before she died.

I am especially grateful for the generous encouragement of Seamus Heaney, at the very beginning of my endeavor.

I wish to thank, in a special way, Marie Němec Banerjee, professor of Russian and Comparative Literature at Smith College and her husband the poet Ron Banerjee for reading the poems with great care, understanding and empathy (coming up with several precious suggestions, such as Fin Amor,) and generously bestowing their academic and professional imprimatur.

Josef Staša read the poems equally carefully, untying several mysteries, such as the word divizna- verbascum, name of an endangered species of plants with tall stems, carrying brilliant yellow and white flowers, native to the Sub-Carpathian Mountains of the poet's childhood.

Marie Foley's faithful and true friendship provided much needed support. Matha Schieve listened patiently to many recapitulations of the significance of Czech history and Agnes' role in it, during our morning walks.

I could not of course, have done any of this without my husband's constant, loving, stabilizing presence. My daughter's Christina's interest in all things Czech, as well as her computer savvy, were invaluable, as was the love and support of all my children and grandchildren, particularly Maria Chiara and Catherine Rose.